Homeowner's Renovation Tips & Log Book

From Planning To Completion

JOEL CANNON

INTRODUCTION

This log book is designed for you to document every step of your project. Whether you're remodeling or upgrading one room in your house, multiple rooms, giving your patio a facelift, re-doing your yard, replacing flooring or even just sprucing up your walls with new paint, keeping a detailed log book can be very useful, especially if something unexpected happens with your project and you need documentation.

As time passes, memories and specifics fade. Should you find yourself in the middle of a contentious situation with your contractors, you don't want to have to start piecing details together without having documentation of solid facts. It's always easier to keep notes as you go.

Sections in this book include:
- Tips and reminders to help with various aspects of your project
- A dot grid page to sketch out designs
- An overview page for project description, budget, ideas, as well as space for inspiration pictures
- 6 detailed pages to note information about potential contractors you contact
- Project details and timeline overview to note start date, contractor's information, budget, estimate details, and more
- 30 pages with fill-in fields for keeping track of daily details including contractor start/end times, description of work started/completed, names of contractors/subcontractors working each day, along with extra space to note progress, conversations, issues, etc.
  NOTE: It's important to fill out these pages on a daily basis. Renovation projects usually involve a lot of moving parts. It can be stressful for a homeowner. Trying to remember details weeks, or even just a few days, after something happens is often too difficult. The sooner you document everything, the easier it will be. Also, remember to take plenty of pictures and/or videos which can serve as proof should the need arise. Plus, photos are nice to have for your own before & after reference.
- 42 blank lined pages. Since every project has a different timeline, these pages can be used as additional daily pages or for extra notes.
- A project recap page to summarize the work done, your review of the contractors, date completed, final cost, and more

Copyright © 2020 Joel Cannon
All rights reserved.

No part of this book may be reproduced, stored in a database or retrieval system or distributed in any form, in whole or in part, by any means, electronic, mechanical, photocopying, recording, or otherwise, without prior written permission from the author.

Tips

Whether this is your first home remodel project or you've been through this before, these tips are always a good reminder.

Planning:
- Figure out your budget. Whatever that amount is, make sure it includes at least 10-30% more for unexpected costs due to delays, changes, or mistakes. Things like paying extra rent in your current home, having to buy more materials, or correcting unforeseen construction issues are just a few of the reasons that could push you over your budget.
- Include professional cleaning services in your budget. Even if you or the contractors do everything possible to minimize the dust and mess that comes with every remodel or upgrade, having a thorough cleaning after the project is completed will probably be necessary. While it's not a good idea to turn on the air conditioner or furnace, especially during the demo, you might want to budget for air duct cleaning also.
- If anyone in your household has health issues, is sensitive to odors, allergic to dust or chemicals, take the necessary precautions. Talk to your contractor about safety procedures and what materials will be used.
- Decide on your target deadline. Leave yourself enough leeway in the event something happens where it can't be completed on time. You may think it's the simplest project and there shouldn't be any issues but there are countless things that can cause delays.
- Unless your project is time-sensitive and critical, planning around weather, when possible, is a good idea. Even simple things like painting are not as convenient to do in the winter if you need to have windows open to air out any odors.
- Prepare yourself and/or your family for the discomfort and inconvenience that comes with most remodeling projects. It can be a stressful time. Organize things as much as possible. Have a plan for temporary living arrangements that may be necessary. Again, accept the fact that remodeling projects often aren't completed on time.
- This may be obvious but it's still worth mentioning. While home remodeling shows on TV are fun to watch, they are far from realistic. Don't expect your real project to be the same as anything you see on TV.
- Spend time looking at ideas and photos for inspiration. Have a clear picture of the results you're expecting. Check local renovation groups on social media. Ask for recommendations for contractors, material ideas, etc. Don't go into this blindly.
- Research any materials that you plan on using in your project (solid surface countertops, tiles, flooring, carpet, paint colors, etc.). Some things to consider would be ease of cleaning, practicality, durability, suitable for the purpose intended, and cost. Picking the best material is really important since you'll probably have it for many years.
- Remember to research the pros and cons for what you're considering. Certain materials may look beautiful but may not be the most practical or functional for your needs.

- Trends come and go. Unless you have an unlimited budget and like remodeling just to keep up with the latest trend, you might want to consider a design, color scheme, and other elements that will withstand the test of time.
- Consider the current layout of the room you're upgrading. Maybe you only planned a facelift but if there are issues with the layout that have always bothered you, this remodel would be the time to fix those problems and design the room that works better for you. Understandably, a remodel with a completely different layout will cost more than just a facelift but it might be worth it in the long run.
- Google, Google, Google. Spend time researching as much as you can now rather than later. Once the project starts, you'll be knee deep in so many things that you may not have the time or the energy to gather necessary information.
- Be ready to compromise or make adjustments if necessary. While you may have your heart set on a certain look for your project, sometimes functional or structural issues may require changes to be made.

Contractors:
- Most states have guidelines, regulations, and laws governing contractors. Before you even start looking for potential contractors, get familiar with what your state requires from contractors but also, what your rights are as a homeowner.
- Make sure you are aware of city building codes and permit requirements.
- There are basically three types of contractors. A *general contractor* is the person who oversees the project and who enters into the contract with the homeowner. A *trade contractor* specializes in a certain part of the project (i.e. flooring, tile, cabinetry, electrical, plumbing, etc.). A *handyman* is usually a person who does smaller jobs and in some states, doesn't fall under the contractor status or rules. Understand the differences and the limits set forth by your state laws.
- Some states have laws that apply to subcontractors versus employees of general contractors. Make sure you check into those laws as they may affect your rights should a problem arise with workmanship, breach of contract, liability, or failure to perform.
- It is strongly suggested you get at least three estimates from contractors. However, sometimes that isn't enough for a variety of reasons. While contacting and meeting with contractors is time consuming, it's better to take your time and hire the best one possible.
- As you meet with potential contractors, make sure anything you discuss is put in writing. For example, if they say they will protect and cover your property (i.e. furniture, adjoining rooms, floors, appliances, etc.) with plastic or another material during demo, get that in writing. They should automatically put that information on their written estimate but not all contractors follow industry guidelines. Plus, sometimes it can be weeks or longer from the time an estimate is done until the work actually begins. Verbal information isn't always remembered correctly by all parties. Having everything in writing can be the difference between a good experience and a nightmare you regret.

- Discuss the specific timeline with the contractor for the various phases of the project. Make notes for the dates of each phase. This will help to know if the project is on track and if you need to make adjustments for any reason.
- If you are purchasing appliances, lighting fixtures, faucets, drapes, etc., a breakdown of the timeline can help you schedule deliveries and make sure have the necessary items ready for the installation phase.
- If you are expected to prep the area in any way prior to the contractor starting work, make sure that is also in writing and fully understood.
- In addition to all of the necessary information on the estimate (price, materials, payment schedule, and whatever else your state's contractor laws require), ask them to sketch out a diagram of your project, if necessary. This is another area where verbal communication and misunderstandings can cause an issue. A picture or sketch is worth a thousand words and helps avoid confusion.
- Make sure the estimate includes who pays for what. Sometimes the contractor will use their industry discount and buy all the materials but other times, they may expect the homeowner to buy certain things. Get those details in writing. If the contractor buys the materials, you might want to ask them if they markup the price and if so, by how much.
- If the contractor doesn't specify, ask what type of payment they accept. If they take credit cards, make sure you ask if they charge a processing fee. You don't want to have surprises.
- Take photos frequently throughout the process. It may seem like overkill but should issues arise with the workmanship or the contractor in any way, you'll be glad you had photos as documentation if you need to prove anything later on. No one likes to think about a lawsuit, but things can happen where that may be necessary.
- Even if you have a general contractor or foreman to oversee the project, that person probably isn't going to be there every minute. It's a good idea for you to frequently monitor the work each day. If you see something that doesn't look right, immediately have them stop and call the person in charge. It's easier to correct something before it's done rather than after.
- Every time you make a payment, the contractor should give you a receipt. If they don't, make sure you ask for one. Keep it with this book or wherever you keep your financial records. You may need it later on. Some home improvements are eligible for tax deductions so it's a good idea to look into that with your CPA or tax preparer.
- Contractors may not tell you everything. Sometimes they're so used to doing things a certain way, or even just one way, that they don't always think to communicate the small details to the homeowner. While you want someone who is willing to work with your ideas, beware of anyone who will agree to everything because sometimes there are solid reasons why your ideas or certain materials may not work. They're supposed to be the professional, the expert, the one who has experience in their trade. It's their responsibility to inform you if there is a better way to do something or at least make you aware of other options and the reasons for them.

- Don't be afraid to ask questions or speak up if you see something that doesn't make sense. Contractors are human. Mistakes happen. Remember, you're the one who has to live with the results. Make sure things are done right the first time.
- Sometimes even with the best plan, you may see something that you wish you could change during the project. As you're interviewing potential contractors, it's a good idea to discuss how they deal with changes if a homeowner wants them.
- The lowest estimate isn't necessarily the best option. On the flip side, the highest estimate doesn't always mean that the contractor is the most experienced or the one that's right for your project. While money is a consideration for most homeowners, finding the right contractor is the most important factor.
- Communication is key. During your search for potential contractors, note which ones are willing to listen to your wants and needs versus which ones appear to only want to do it their way. There will be a lot of times during the project that being able to communicate and understand each other is critical.
- Get references. Read reviews. Look at their social media and/or website. If your state has licensing requirements, check with the organization or government office that regulates contractors. Check their license status. See if they've had any complaints filed against them. Check the Better Business Bureau. Yes, this can be a lot of work but better safe than sorry because even the smallest mistakes can cause a major expense.
- Ask what the warranty is on workmanship and/or materials. Get that in writing.
- Doorways, stairs, floors, walls, etc. in other parts of your house may be damaged during a demo or remodel. Make sure the contract specifies whose responsibility it is to repair or pay for that damage.
- NEVER EVER take just one or two sources' opinions about anything. Just like most industries, contractors will have a lot of different opinions. Don't be surprised if they contradict each other. Educate yourself so you can go into your project with as much knowledge as possible.
- The best contractor will work *with* you, not just *for* you. But remember, it's your house. Your project. Your money. You have to be happy with the results.

Notes: _____

_____

_____

_____

_____

Project Overview

Today's Date: _____

Brief Project Description: _____

_____

_____

_____

_____

_____

Budget: _____   Desired start/completion dates: _____

Use this space for inspiration photos.

Potential Contractors

Today's Date: _____   Project: _____

1st Potential Contractor   **Hired?** ☐ Yes   ☐ No

Company: _____

General Contractor or Specific Trade: _____

Contact Person: _____   Contractor License #: _____

Insured? ☐ Yes ☐ No   Bonded? ☐ Yes ☐ No   Other info: _____

Do they use employees or subcontractors? _____

Phone: _____   Email: _____

Address: _____

Website (if any): _____

How did you hear about them? _____

Date contacted: _____   ☐ Phone call ☐ Email ☐ Text ☐ FB message

If you left a message, did they reply? ☐ Yes ☐ No   If yes, when? _____

Was an estimate scheduled?   ☐ Yes ☐ No   If yes, when? _____

Did they show up on time?   ☐ Yes ☐ No   If no, did they call? ☐ Yes ☐ No

Were they a no-show?   ☐ Yes ☐ No   Second chance? ☐ Yes ☐ No

Did they provide a written estimate? ☐ Yes ☐ No   Total price: _____

How did you receive it? ☐ Email ☐ Text ☐ Facebook message ☐ Other _____

Do they require a down payment? ☐ Yes ☐ No   How much? _____

Type of payment they accept? ☐ Credit card ☐ Personal check ☐ Cash ☐ Other _____

Are they available for your timeline? ☐ Yes ☐ No   Would you use them? ☐ Yes ☐ No

Things you liked/disliked about them and other notes: _____

_____

_____

Today's Date: _____   Project: _____

2nd Potential Contractor   **Hired?** ☐ Yes   ☐ No

Company: _____

General Contractor or Specific Trade: _____

Contact Person: _____   Contractor License #: _____

Insured? ☐ Yes   ☐ No   Bonded? ☐ Yes   ☐ No   Other info: _____

Do they use employees or subcontractors? _____

Phone: _____   Email: _____

Address: _____

Website (if any): _____

How did you hear about them? _____

Date contacted: _____   ☐ Phone call ☐ Email ☐ Text ☐ FB message

If you left a message, did they reply? ☐ Yes   ☐ No   If yes, when? _____

Was an estimate scheduled?   ☐ Yes   ☐ No   If yes, when? _____

Did they show up on time?   ☐ Yes   ☐ No   If no, did they call? ☐ Yes   ☐ No

Were they a no-show?   ☐ Yes   ☐ No   Second chance? ☐ Yes   ☐ No

Did they provide a written estimate? ☐ Yes   ☐ No   Total price: _____

How did you receive it? ☐ Email   ☐ Text   ☐ Facebook message   ☐ Other _____

Do they require a down payment?   ☐ Yes   ☐ No   How much? _____

Type of payment they accept? ☐ Credit card   ☐ Personal check   ☐ Cash   ☐ Other _____

Are they available for your timeline? ☐ Yes   ☐ No   Would you use them? ☐ Yes   ☐ No

Things you liked/disliked about them and other notes: _____

_____

_____

Today's Date: _____   Project: _____

3rd Potential Contractor   Hired? ☐ Yes ☐ No

Company: _____

General Contractor or Specific Trade: _____

Contact Person: _____ Contractor License #: _____

Insured? ☐ Yes ☐ No   Bonded? ☐ Yes ☐ No   Other info: _____

Do they use employees or subcontractors? _____

Phone: _____   Email: _____

Address: _____

Website (if any): _____

How did you hear about them? _____

Date contacted: _____ ☐ Phone call ☐ Email ☐ Text ☐ FB message

If you left a message, did they reply? ☐ Yes ☐ No   If yes, when? _____

Was an estimate scheduled? ☐ Yes ☐ No   If yes, when? _____

Did they show up on time? ☐ Yes ☐ No   If no, did they call? ☐ Yes ☐ No

Were they a no-show? ☐ Yes ☐ No   Second chance? ☐ Yes ☐ No

Did they provide a written estimate? ☐ Yes ☐ No   Total price: _____

How did you receive it? ☐ Email ☐ Text ☐ Facebook message ☐ Other _____

Do they require a down payment? ☐ Yes ☐ No   How much? _____

Type of payment they accept? ☐ Credit card ☐ Personal check ☐ Cash ☐ Other _____

Are they available for your timeline? ☐ Yes ☐ No   Would you use them? ☐ Yes ☐ No

Things you liked/disliked about them and other notes: _____

_____

_____

_____

Today's Date: _____ Project: _____

4th Potential Contractor   **Hired?** ☐ Yes ☐ No

Company: _____

General Contractor or Specific Trade: _____

Contact Person: _____ Contractor License #: _____

Insured? ☐ Yes ☐ No   Bonded? ☐ Yes ☐ No   Other info: _____

Do they use employees or subcontractors? _____

Phone: _____ Email: _____

Address: _____

Website (if any): _____

How did you hear about them? _____

Date contacted: _____ ☐ Phone call ☐ Email ☐ Text ☐ FB message

If you left a message, did they reply? ☐ Yes ☐ No   If yes, when? _____

Was an estimate scheduled?   ☐ Yes ☐ No   If yes, when? _____

Did they show up on time?   ☐ Yes ☐ No   If no, did they call? ☐ Yes ☐ No

Were they a no-show?   ☐ Yes ☐ No   Second chance? ☐ Yes ☐ No

Did they provide a written estimate? ☐ Yes ☐ No   Total price: _____

How did you receive it? ☐ Email ☐ Text ☐ Facebook message ☐ Other _____

Do they require a down payment? ☐ Yes ☐ No   How much? _____

Type of payment they accept? ☐ Credit card ☐ Personal check ☐ Cash ☐ Other _____

Are they available for your timeline? ☐ Yes ☐ No   Would you use them? ☐ Yes ☐ No

Things you liked/disliked about them and other notes: _____

_____

_____

_____

Today's Date: _____   Project: _____

5th Potential Contractor   **Hired?** ☐ Yes   ☐ No

Company: _____

General Contractor or Specific Trade: _____

Contact Person: _____   Contractor License #: _____

Insured? ☐ Yes ☐ No   Bonded? ☐ Yes ☐ No   Other info: _____

Do they use employees or subcontractors? _____

Phone: _____   Email: _____

Address: _____

Website (if any): _____

How did you hear about them? _____

Date contacted: _____ ☐ Phone call ☐ Email ☐ Text ☐ FB message

If you left a message, did they reply? ☐ Yes ☐ No   If yes, when? _____

Was an estimate scheduled?   ☐ Yes ☐ No   If yes, when? _____

Did they show up on time?   ☐ Yes ☐ No   If no, did they call? ☐ Yes ☐ No

Were they a no-show?   ☐ Yes ☐ No   Second chance? ☐ Yes ☐ No

Did they provide a written estimate? ☐ Yes ☐ No   Total price: _____

How did you receive it? ☐ Email ☐ Text ☐ Facebook message ☐ Other _____

Do they require a down payment? ☐ Yes ☐ No   How much? _____

Type of payment they accept? ☐ Credit card ☐ Personal check ☐ Cash ☐ Other _____

Are they available for your timeline? ☐ Yes ☐ No   Would you use them? ☐ Yes ☐ No

Things you liked/disliked about them and other notes: _____

_____

_____

Today's Date: _____ Project: _____

6th Potential Contractor   **Hired?** ☐ Yes ☐ No

Company: _____

General Contractor or Specific Trade: _____

Contact Person: _____ Contractor License #: _____

Insured? ☐ Yes ☐ No   Bonded? ☐ Yes ☐ No   Other info: _____

Do they use employees or subcontractors? _____

Phone: _____ Email: _____

Address: _____

Website (if any): _____

How did you hear about them? _____

Date contacted: _____ ☐ Phone call ☐ Email ☐ Text ☐ FB message

If you left a message, did they reply? ☐ Yes ☐ No   If yes, when? _____

Was an estimate scheduled? ☐ Yes ☐ No   If yes, when? _____

Did they show up on time? ☐ Yes ☐ No   If no, did they call? ☐ Yes ☐ No

Were they a no-show? ☐ Yes ☐ No   Second chance? ☐ Yes ☐ No

Did they provide a written estimate? ☐ Yes ☐ No   Total price: _____

How did you receive it? ☐ Email ☐ Text ☐ Facebook message ☐ Other _____

Do they require a down payment? ☐ Yes ☐ No   How much? _____

Type of payment they accept? ☐ Credit card ☐ Personal check ☐ Cash ☐ Other _____

Are they available for your timeline? ☐ Yes ☐ No   Would you use them? ☐ Yes ☐ No

Things you liked/disliked about them and other notes: _____

_____

_____

_____

Project Details
& Timeline

PROJECT DETAILS & TIMELINE

Overview

Project description: _____

Contractor's name: _____ Date hired: _____

Scheduled start date and time: _____

If original start date/time was changed, did the contractor inform you? ☐ Yes ☐ No

What was the reason for the change? _____

If rescheduled, what is the new start date and time? _____

Date and time work actually started: _____

Did the contractor come or did they send other workers instead? _____

Demo Phase

If demo is needed, did they protect your property (i.e. furniture, walls, floors, stairs, appliances, etc.) with appropriate material? ☐ Yes ☐ No

Describe demo phase in as much detail as you can: _____

_____

_____

_____

_____

_____

(This information may be needed should any issues or damage arise in other areas due to their negligence.)

How long did the demo take? _____ Did it match the estimate time? ☐ Yes ☐ No

If not, what were the reasons? Were there unforeseen issues? Describe: _____

_____

After the demo, did they clean up the area to your satisfaction? ☐ Yes ☐ No

If not, what were the issues? _____

_____

Additional notes: _____

Daily Details

Daily Details

Today's date: _____   Time work started: _____   Time ended: _____

Describe what work is scheduled to be done today: _____

_____

_____

_____

_____

Names of those working: _____

_____

Any subcontractors? ☐ Yes   ☐ No   Company name: _____

Did the scheduled work get done as planned today? ☐ Yes   ☐ No

Progress, notes, issues: _____

_____

_____

_____

_____

_____

_____

_____

_____

_____

_____

_____

Daily Details

Today's date: _____   Time work started: _____   Time ended: _____

Describe what work is scheduled to be done today: _____

_____

_____

_____

_____

Names of those working: _____

_____

Any subcontractors? ☐ Yes   ☐ No   Company name: _____

Did the scheduled work get done as planned today? ☐ Yes   ☐ No

Progress, notes, issues: _____

_____

_____

_____

_____

_____

_____

_____

_____

_____

_____

_____

_____

Daily Details

Today's date: _____ Time work started: _____ Time ended: _____

Describe what work is scheduled to be done today: _____

_____

_____

_____

_____

Names of those working: _____

_____

Any subcontractors? ☐ Yes ☐ No   Company name: _____

Did the scheduled work get done as planned today? ☐ Yes ☐ No

Progress, notes, issues: _____

_____

_____

_____

_____

_____

_____

_____

_____

_____

_____

_____

Daily Details

Today's date: _____ Time work started: _____ Time ended: _____

Describe what work is scheduled to be done today: _____

_____

_____

_____

_____

Names of those working: _____

_____

Any subcontractors? ☐ Yes ☐ No   Company name: _____

Did the scheduled work get done as planned today? ☐ Yes ☐ No

Progress, notes, issues: _____

_____

_____

_____

_____

_____

_____

_____

_____

_____

_____

_____

Daily Details

Today's date: _____   Time work started: _____   Time ended: _____

Describe what work is scheduled to be done today: _____

_____

_____

_____

_____

Names of those working: _____

_____

Any subcontractors? ☐ Yes   ☐ No   Company name: _____

Did the scheduled work get done as planned today? ☐ Yes   ☐ No

Progress, notes, issues: _____

_____

_____

_____

_____

_____

_____

_____

_____

_____

_____

_____

Daily Details

Today's date: _____   Time work started: _____   Time ended: _____

Describe what work is scheduled to be done today: _____

_____

_____

_____

_____

Names of those working: _____

_____

Any subcontractors? ☐ Yes   ☐ No   Company name: _____

Did the scheduled work get done as planned today? ☐ Yes   ☐ No

Progress, notes, issues: _____

_____

_____

_____

_____

_____

_____

_____

_____

_____

_____

_____

Daily Details

Today's date: _____ Time work started: _____ Time ended: _____

Describe what work is scheduled to be done today: _____

_____

_____

_____

_____

Names of those working: _____

_____

Any subcontractors? ☐ Yes ☐ No   Company name: _____

Did the scheduled work get done as planned today? ☐ Yes ☐ No

Progress, notes, issues: _____

_____

_____

_____

_____

_____

_____

_____

_____

_____

_____

_____

Daily Details

Today's date: _____ Time work started: _____ Time ended: _____

Describe what work is scheduled to be done today: _____

_____

_____

_____

_____

Names of those working: _____

_____

Any subcontractors? ☐ Yes ☐ No   Company name: _____

Did the scheduled work get done as planned today? ☐ Yes ☐ No

Progress, notes, issues: _____

_____

_____

_____

_____

_____

_____

_____

_____

_____

_____

_____

Daily Details

Today's date: _____   Time work started: _____   Time ended: _____

Describe what work is scheduled to be done today: _____

_____

_____

_____

_____

Names of those working: _____

_____

Any subcontractors? ☐ Yes ☐ No   Company name: _____

Did the scheduled work get done as planned today? ☐ Yes ☐ No

Progress, notes, issues: _____

_____

_____

_____

_____

_____

_____

_____

_____

_____

_____

_____

Daily Details

Today's date: _____   Time work started: _____   Time ended: _____

Describe what work is scheduled to be done today: _____

_____

_____

_____

_____

Names of those working: _____

_____

Any subcontractors? ☐ Yes   ☐ No   Company name: _____

Did the scheduled work get done as planned today? ☐ Yes   ☐ No

Progress, notes, issues: _____

_____

_____

_____

_____

_____

_____

_____

_____

_____

_____

_____

_____

Daily Details

Today's date: _____   Time work started: _____   Time ended: _____

Describe what work is scheduled to be done today: _____

_____

_____

_____

_____

Names of those working: _____

_____

Any subcontractors? ☐ Yes   ☐ No   Company name: _____

Did the scheduled work get done as planned today? ☐ Yes   ☐ No

Progress, notes, issues: _____

_____

_____

_____

_____

_____

_____

_____

_____

_____

_____

_____

Daily Details

Today's date: _____ Time work started: _____ Time ended: _____

Describe what work is scheduled to be done today: _____

_____

_____

_____

_____

Names of those working: _____

_____

Any subcontractors? ☐ Yes ☐ No   Company name: _____

Did the scheduled work get done as planned today? ☐ Yes ☐ No

Progress, notes, issues: _____

_____

_____

_____

_____

_____

_____

_____

_____

_____

_____

_____

_____

Daily Details

Today's date: _____   Time work started: _____   Time ended: _____

Describe what work is scheduled to be done today: _____

_____

_____

_____

_____

Names of those working: _____

_____

Any subcontractors? ☐ Yes   ☐ No   Company name: _____

Did the scheduled work get done as planned today? ☐ Yes   ☐ No

Progress, notes, issues: _____

_____

_____

_____

_____

_____

_____

_____

_____

_____

_____

_____

Daily Details

Today's date: _____   Time work started: _____   Time ended: _____

Describe what work is scheduled to be done today: _____

_____

_____

_____

_____

Names of those working: _____

_____

Any subcontractors? ☐ Yes   ☐ No   Company name: _____

Did the scheduled work get done as planned today? ☐ Yes   ☐ No

Progress, notes, issues: _____

_____

_____

_____

_____

_____

_____

_____

_____

_____

_____

_____

Daily Details

Today's date: _____ Time work started: _____ Time ended: _____

Describe what work is scheduled to be done today: _____

_____

_____

_____

_____

Names of those working: _____

_____

Any subcontractors? ☐ Yes ☐ No   Company name: _____

Did the scheduled work get done as planned today? ☐ Yes ☐ No

Progress, notes, issues: _____

_____

_____

_____

_____

_____

_____

_____

_____

_____

_____

_____

Daily Details

Today's date: _____ Time work started: _____ Time ended: _____

Describe what work is scheduled to be done today: _____

_____

_____

_____

_____

Names of those working: _____

_____

Any subcontractors? ☐ Yes ☐ No   Company name: _____

Did the scheduled work get done as planned today? ☐ Yes ☐ No

Progress, notes, issues: _____

_____

_____

_____

_____

_____

_____

_____

_____

_____

_____

_____

Daily Details

Today's date: _____   Time work started: _____   Time ended: _____

Describe what work is scheduled to be done today: _____

_____

_____

_____

_____

Names of those working: _____

_____

Any subcontractors? ☐ Yes   ☐ No   Company name: _____

Did the scheduled work get done as planned today? ☐ Yes   ☐ No

Progress, notes, issues: _____

_____

_____

_____

_____

_____

_____

_____

_____

_____

_____

_____

Daily Details

Today's date: _____ Time work started: _____ Time ended: _____

Describe what work is scheduled to be done today: _____

_____

_____

_____

_____

Names of those working: _____

_____

Any subcontractors? ☐ Yes ☐ No   Company name: _____

Did the scheduled work get done as planned today? ☐ Yes ☐ No

Progress, notes, issues: _____

_____

_____

_____

_____

_____

_____

_____

_____

_____

_____

_____

_____

Daily Details

Today's date: _____ Time work started: _____ Time ended: _____

Describe what work is scheduled to be done today: _____

_____

_____

_____

_____

Names of those working: _____

_____

Any subcontractors? ☐ Yes   ☐ No   Company name: _____

Did the scheduled work get done as planned today? ☐ Yes   ☐ No

Progress, notes, issues: _____

_____

_____

_____

_____

_____

_____

_____

_____

_____

_____

_____

Daily Details

Today's date: _____   Time work started: _____   Time ended: _____

Describe what work is scheduled to be done today: _____

_____

_____

_____

_____

Names of those working: _____

_____

Any subcontractors? ☐ Yes   ☐ No   Company name: _____

Did the scheduled work get done as planned today? ☐ Yes   ☐ No

Progress, notes, issues: _____

_____

_____

_____

_____

_____

_____

_____

_____

_____

_____

_____

Daily Details

Today's date: _____   Time work started: _____   Time ended: _____

Describe what work is scheduled to be done today: _____

_____

_____

_____

_____

Names of those working: _____

_____

Any subcontractors? ☐ Yes   ☐ No   Company name: _____

Did the scheduled work get done as planned today? ☐ Yes   ☐ No

Progress, notes, issues: _____

_____

_____

_____

_____

_____

_____

_____

_____

_____

_____

_____

_____

Daily Details

Today's date: _____ Time work started: _____ Time ended: _____

Describe what work is scheduled to be done today: _____

_____

_____

_____

_____

Names of those working: _____

_____

Any subcontractors? ☐ Yes   ☐ No   Company name: _____

Did the scheduled work get done as planned today? ☐ Yes   ☐ No

Progress, notes, issues: _____

_____

_____

_____

_____

_____

_____

_____

_____

_____

_____

_____

Daily Details

Today's date: _____   Time work started: _____   Time ended: _____

Describe what work is scheduled to be done today: _____

_____

_____

_____

_____

Names of those working: _____

_____

Any subcontractors? ☐ Yes   ☐ No   Company name: _____

Did the scheduled work get done as planned today? ☐ Yes   ☐ No

Progress, notes, issues: _____

_____

_____

_____

_____

_____

_____

_____

_____

_____

_____

_____

_____

Daily Details

Today's date: _____   Time work started: _____   Time ended: _____

Describe what work is scheduled to be done today: _____

_____

_____

_____

_____

Names of those working: _____

_____

Any subcontractors? ☐ Yes   ☐ No   Company name: _____

Did the scheduled work get done as planned today? ☐ Yes   ☐ No

Progress, notes, issues: _____

_____

_____

_____

_____

_____

_____

_____

_____

_____

_____

_____

_____

Daily Details

Today's date: _____   Time work started: _____   Time ended: _____

Describe what work is scheduled to be done today: _____

_____

_____

_____

_____

Names of those working: _____

_____

Any subcontractors? ☐ Yes   ☐ No   Company name: _____

Did the scheduled work get done as planned today? ☐ Yes   ☐ No

Progress, notes, issues: _____

_____

_____

_____

_____

_____

_____

_____

_____

_____

_____

_____

Daily Details

Today's date: _____   Time work started: _____   Time ended: _____

Describe what work is scheduled to be done today: _____

_____

_____

_____

_____

Names of those working: _____

_____

Any subcontractors? ☐ Yes   ☐ No   Company name: _____

Did the scheduled work get done as planned today? ☐ Yes   ☐ No

Progress, notes, issues: _____

_____

_____

_____

_____

_____

_____

_____

_____

_____

_____

_____

_____

Daily Details

Today's date: _____ Time work started: _____ Time ended: _____

Describe what work is scheduled to be done today: _____

_____

_____

_____

_____

Names of those working: _____

_____

Any subcontractors? ☐ Yes ☐ No   Company name: _____

Did the scheduled work get done as planned today? ☐ Yes ☐ No

Progress, notes, issues: _____

_____

_____

_____

_____

_____

_____

_____

_____

_____

_____

_____

Daily Details

Today's date: _____   Time work started: _____   Time ended: _____

Describe what work is scheduled to be done today: _____

_____

_____

_____

_____

Names of those working: _____

_____

Any subcontractors? ☐ Yes   ☐ No   Company name: _____

Did the scheduled work get done as planned today? ☐ Yes   ☐ No

Progress, notes, issues: _____

_____

_____

_____

_____

_____

_____

_____

_____

_____

_____

_____

_____

Daily Details

Today's date: _____ Time work started: _____ Time ended: _____

Describe what work is scheduled to be done today: _____

_____

_____

_____

_____

Names of those working: _____

_____

Any subcontractors? ☐ Yes ☐ No   Company name: _____

Did the scheduled work get done as planned today? ☐ Yes ☐ No

Progress, notes, issues: _____

_____

_____

_____

_____

_____

_____

_____

_____

_____

_____

Daily Details

Today's date: _____   Time work started: _____   Time ended: _____

Describe what work is scheduled to be done today: _____

_____

_____

_____

_____

Names of those working: _____

_____

Any subcontractors? ☐ Yes ☐ No   Company name: _____

Did the scheduled work get done as planned today? ☐ Yes ☐ No

Progress, notes, issues: _____

_____

_____

_____

_____

_____

_____

_____

_____

_____

_____

_____

_____

Additional daily details, notes, etc.

Additional daily details, notes, etc.

Additional daily details, notes, etc.

Additional daily details, notes, etc.

Additional daily details, notes, etc.

Additional daily details, notes, etc.

Additional daily details, notes, etc.

Additional daily details, notes, etc.

Additional daily details, notes, etc.

Additional daily details, notes, etc.

Additional daily details, notes, etc.

Additional daily details, notes, etc.

Additional daily details, notes, etc.

Additional daily details, notes, etc.

Additional daily details, notes, etc.

Additional daily details, notes, etc.

Additional daily details, notes, etc.

Additional daily details, notes, etc.

Additional daily details, notes, etc.

Additional daily details, notes, etc.

Additional daily details, notes, etc.

Additional daily details, notes, etc.

Additional daily details, notes, etc.

Additional daily details, notes, etc.

Additional daily details, notes, etc.

Additional daily details, notes, etc.

Additional daily details, notes, etc.

Additional daily details, notes, etc.

Additional daily details, notes, etc.

Additional daily details, notes, etc.

Additional daily details, notes, etc.

Additional daily details, notes, etc.

Additional daily details, notes, etc.

Additional daily details, notes, etc.

Additional daily details, notes, etc.

Additional daily details, notes, etc.

Additional daily details, notes, etc.

Additional daily details, notes, etc.

Additional daily details, notes, etc.

Additional daily details, notes, etc.

Additional daily details, notes, etc.

Additional daily details, notes, etc.

Project Recap

Project Recap

Was the project completed on time? ☐ Yes ☐ No   Was it on budget? ☐ Yes ☐ No

If no to either, describe issues and the difference in the total cost: _____

_____

_____

_____

Were you satisfied with the work overall? ☐ Yes ☐ No

If no, explain: _____

_____

_____

If there were issues, did the contractor agree or attempt to resolve them? ☐ Yes ☐ No

If yes, were the issues fixed to your satisfaction? ☐ Yes ☐ No

If yes, how/when? _____

_____

_____

If no, explain: _____

_____

_____

If issues weren't resolved, what other action will you take? _____

_____

_____

What method of payment did you use? _____   Dates: _____

_____

Would you use this contractor again or recommend them to anyone else? ☐ Yes ☐ No

Made in the USA
Las Vegas, NV
05 April 2025